Visit and Learn

The Black Hills

by Rachel Bithell

FOCUS
READERS.

BEACON

www.focusreaders.com

Focus Readers is distributed by North Star Editions:
sales@northstareditions.com | 888-417-0195

Produced for Focus Readers by Red Line Editorial.

Photographs ©: Shutterstock Images, cover, 1, 4, 7, 8, 11, 13, 19, 20–21, 22, 25, 27, 28–29; Stephen Groves/AP Images, 14; Joel Ebert/Rapid City Journal/AP Images, 17

Library of Congress Cataloging-in-Publication Data
Names: Bithell, Rachel, author.
Title: The Black Hills / by Rachel Bithell.
Description: Lake Elmo, MN : Focus Readers, [2024] | Series: Visit and
  learn | Includes bibliographical references and index. | Audience:
  Grades 2-3
Identifiers: LCCN 2022058543 (print) | LCCN 2022058544 (ebook) | ISBN
  9781637396155 (hardcover) | ISBN 9781637396728 (paperback) | ISBN
  9781637397824 (pdf) | ISBN 9781637397299 (ebook)
Subjects: LCSH: Black Hills (S.D. and Wyo.)--History--Juvenile literature.
Classification: LCC F657.B6 B48 2024 (print) | LCC F657.B6 (ebook) | DDC
  978.3/9--dc23/eng/20221213
LC record available at https://lccn.loc.gov/2022058543
LC ebook record available at https://lccn.loc.gov/2022058544

Printed in the United States of America
Mankato, MN
082023

About the Author

Rachel Bithell writes fiction and nonfiction for kids and their caregivers. She loves the Black Hills for their remarkable scenery, history, and activities. If she's not writing or helping someone with homework, she will probably be reading a book or trying to help something grow in her yard.

Table of Contents

Chapter 1

Sacred Mountains

The Lakota call them *Pahá Sápa*. That means "Black Hills." To the Lakota, they are more than hills. They are a **sacred** place.

The Black Hills are a group of mountains in South Dakota.

 Indigenous peoples have lived in the Black Hills for thousands of years.

Pine forests cover the area. The trees are dark. They make the mountains look black.

The Black Hills formed 65 to 70 million years ago. Pressure grew inside the earth. Slowly, it pushed up layers of rock. Over time, the layers rose thousands

Did You Know?

Black Elk Peak is 7,242 feet (2,207 m) tall. It is the highest point between the Rocky Mountains and the Atlantic Ocean.

A watchtower on Black Elk Peak offers amazing views of the Black Hills.

of feet. This made mountains. They rise from flat plains. People come from around the world to see their beauty.

Chapter 2

Battles and Broken Treaties

People first came to the Black Hills approximately 11,000 years ago. Many **Indigenous** peoples have lived there. The Cheyenne, Arapaho, and Lakota are some of these groups.

 An Indigenous man wears traditional clothing while performing a dance in the Black Hills.

White settlers began arriving in the 1800s. They brought diseases with them. Indigenous people had never faced these diseases. So, their bodies could not fight them. Many Indigenous people died.

Settlers also killed many bison. Indigenous people relied on bison for food. They also used the animals to make clothes and shelter.

Sometimes fighting broke out between the two groups. The settlers asked the US government

> By the early 1900s, white settlers had killed nearly all the bison in North America.

for help. The government made a **treaty** in 1868. It was with the Lakota and their **allies**. The treaty said only the Lakota could use the Black Hills. In return, white settlers could travel safely in other places.

In 1874, gold was found in the Black Hills. White settlers poured in. The US government broke the treaty. It took the Black Hills for white settlers. It forced Indigenous peoples to leave.

Some settlers wanted to attract **tourists**. They built businesses

Did You Know?

Mount Rushmore includes a hidden tunnel. The door is behind Lincoln's head. Visitors cannot go inside.

Mount Rushmore shows the faces of George Washington, Thomas Jefferson, Theodore Roosevelt, and Abraham Lincoln.

near lakes, hot springs, and caves. State and national parks were created in the 1900s. So was Mount Rushmore. People carved the faces of four US presidents into a cliff. The work was finished in 1941.

Chapter 3

The Black Hills Today

In 1980, the US Supreme Court made a decision. It said the United States took the Black Hills illegally. The court told the US government to pay the Lakota Nation more than $100 million.

Indigenous protesters want the United States to return the Black Hills to the Lakota people.

However, the Lakota did not want the money. They wanted the Black Hills. Many Lakota are still working to get them back. The US government has kept the money in a bank. By 2022, it was worth nearly $2 billion.

Today, thousands of Indigenous people live in the Black Hills. They preserve and share their **culture** and history. Artists paint, sew, and bead. Elders record their stories. Students learn to speak Lakota.

 Lakota artist Donald Montileaux works on drawings of bison.

People of all ages dance and play drums.

Many of the settlers' towns still stand. Now they are home to ranches and businesses. But some towns show signs of their past.

Deadwood has museums about its mining days. The city of Lead also has a history of mining. The city once had the biggest gold mine in North America. To the west of Custer is a **ghost town**. It is called Four Mile. It has many buildings from the 1800s.

Did You Know?

The Homestake Mine in Lead is now a lab. Scientists work 4,850 feet (1,478 m) below ground.

The Homestake Mine in the city of Lead closed in 2002.

Rapid City is the largest Black Hills city. It offers arts, museums, and parks. One park is called Storybook Island. Statues show events from children's books. The park has many life-size scenes.

Mammoth Site

Approximately 26,000 years ago, a group of mammoths died. They were trapped in a large hole. Over time, earth covered their bodies.

In 1974, a worker was digging. He saw something white. It looked like a big bone. It was a mammoth tusk.

Scientists started digging in the area. They have found more than 1,200 **fossils**. They are still finding more. More than 60 of these fossils are from mammoths. Some are from smaller animals.

Today, scientists teach visitors about fossils at the Mammoth Site.

African elephant 3.4m

Woolly mammoth
Asian elephant 3m

Pygmy mammoth 1.8m

Chapter 4

A Place to Learn and Play

Millions of people visit the Black Hills every year. They come to learn and have fun. Visitors can learn about Indigenous culture. For example, a large mountain carving honors Crazy Horse.

The Crazy Horse Memorial is still being carved.

He was a Lakota leader. The Journey Museum has many artifacts. Some are 10,000 years old. The Black Hills **Powwow** happens in October. People gather to sing, play drums, and dance.

Many visitors spend time outdoors. Hikers and bikers enjoy hundreds of miles of trails. The views are a treat for campers, too. People fish, boat, and swim in lakes and rivers. Trails for skiing are open in winter.

 Hiking is a popular activity in the Black Hills.

Animal lovers can see wildlife. Many bison graze in Custer State Park. Bear Country USA has bears, wolves, and mountain lions. The animals there are free to roam.

Visitors stay in their cars. They see the animals as they drive through. Reptile Gardens has 225 kinds of reptiles. That's the most of any zoo in the world. Visitors can walk with giant tortoises.

Jewel Cave is one of the longest caves in the world. Its name comes

Did You Know?

Reptile Gardens opened in 1937. The owner often hid a snake under his hat. It surprised visitors.

Visitors can see beautiful rock formations at Wind Cave National Park.

from the sparkling rocks on its walls. Wind Cave is a national park. Breezes blow through the cave's entrance. People can tour these caves. They can also learn about the area's history.

FOCUS ON
The Black Hills

Write your answers on a separate piece of paper.

1. Write a paragraph that explains the main ideas of Chapter 3.

2. Do you think the Black Hills should be returned to the Lakota Nation? Why or why not?

3. What is the largest city in the Black Hills?
   - **A.** Deadwood
   - **B.** Custer
   - **C.** Rapid City

4. Why do you think white settlers in the Black Hills wanted to attract tourists?
   - **A.** Tourists would be good company.
   - **B.** Tourists would spend money at their businesses.
   - **C.** Tourists might decide to move to the Black Hills.

5. What does **attract** mean in this book?

*Some settlers wanted to **attract** tourists. They built businesses near lakes, hot springs, and caves.*

    A. to drive a boat or car

    B. to make others want to come near

    C. to spend time in a warm place

6. What does **preserve** mean in this book?

*They **preserve** and share their culture and history. Artists paint, sew, and bead. Elders record their stories.*

    A. to make sure others can't get something

    B. to give gifts to another person

    C. to protect something so it is not lost

Answer key on page 32.

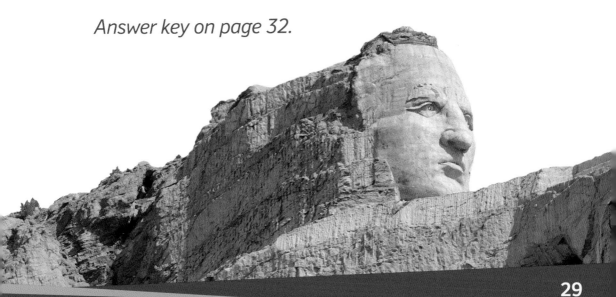

Glossary

allies

Nations or people that are on the same side during a war.

culture

The way a group of people live; their customs, beliefs, and laws.

fossils

Parts of an animal or plant that remain preserved in rock.

ghost town

A city that has been empty for many years, usually with old buildings that are still standing.

Indigenous

Native to a region, or belonging to ancestors who lived in a region before colonists arrived.

powwow

An event celebrating Indigenous cultures. It includes a grand entry, singing, drumming, and dancing.

sacred

Having spiritual or religious meaning.

tourists

People who visit an area for fun or enjoyment.

treaty

An official agreement between groups or countries.

To Learn More

BOOKS

Bird, F. A. *Sioux*. Minneapolis: Abdo Publishing, 2022.

Rathburn, Betsy. *South Dakota*. Minneapolis: Bellwether Media, 2022.

Walsh, Helen Evans. *South Dakota*. Minneapolis: Abdo Publishing, 2022.

NOTE TO EDUCATORS

Visit **www.focusreaders.com** to find lesson plans, activities, links, and other resources related to this title.

Index

A
Arapaho people, 9
artists, 16

B
bison, 10, 25
Black Elk Peak, 6

C
caves, 13, 26–27
Cheyenne people, 9
Crazy Horse, 23–24

F
forests, 6
fossils, 20

G
ghost towns, 18
gold, 12, 18

L
Lakota people, 5, 9, 11,
   15–17, 24

M
Mammoth Site, 20
mining, 18
Mount Rushmore, 12–13

P
powwow, 24

R
Rapid City, 19
Reptile Gardens, 26

S
settlers, 10–12, 17
Supreme Court, 15

T
treaties, 11–12

Answer Key: 1. Answers will vary; **2.** Answers will vary; **3.** C; **4.** B; **5.** B; **6.** C